A LUNDY

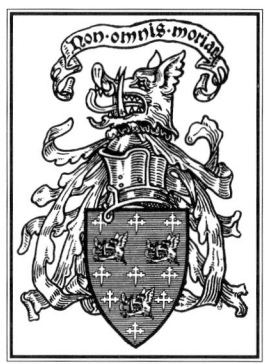

A
LUNDY
ALBUM

MYRTLE

LANGHAM

New Third Edition published by M.S. Langham (Ternstrom), jointly with
The Landmark Trust, Lundy EX39 2LY. 1995

First Edition published privately by M.S. Langham, 1980
Second Edition (Revised), 1987
New (Third) Edition, 1995

ISBN 0 9523062 1 2

The detail for the title page is taken from a drawing by Violet Heaven in her
photograph album.

Cover photograph: Tennis on the Lawn, 1888

Further information about the Heaven family can be found in:
M.S. Langham: *The Heaven Family of Lundy 1836–1916*
Transactions of the Devonshire Assn. 118, 1986

Produced by Alan Sutton Publishing Ltd,
Phoenix Mill, Far Thrupp, Stroud, Glos.
Printed in Great Britain by
Hartnolls, Bodmin, Cornwall.

Foreword to New (Third) Edition

This book is based on the Heaven family photographs, diaries and letters and on the *Lundy Log* and family history written by Mrs M.C.H. Heaven. Miss Eileen Heaven lent me all these for the purpose of this work, and she was very patient in answering my questions – but for her kindness and interest the book would not have been possible.

My aim has been to describe as nearly as possible the island and the people living there during the years that the Heaven family owned Lundy (1836–1917). What distinguished this period from any other in the history of the island is that the owner made Lundy the family home.

This made for an unprecedented period of stability and continuity. The supposition that such an era was also a time of great prosperity is unfortunately unfounded. Lundy never paid its way; it carried mortgages after 1844, and there were very severe problems in trying to match the modest family income to the outgoings for the island and the household. This struggle undoubtedly involved sacrifices, which must have been sustained by their love for the island.

When William Hudson Heaven arrived on Lundy in 1836 all he found there of substance was the lighthouse, the farmhouse, and the castle. The graceful house in Millcombe with gardens and trees, the divisions of the fields, the shape of the farm and its buildings, the church, the quarries, are evidence of their efforts both to enhance the island and to try to make it productive. The island as it is now has largely been shaped by the years of Heaven ownership – their memorial is not only on their gravestones, but all around us.

I am happy that this new edition, issued in conjunction with the Landmark Trust, gives me the opportunity to improve the photographic reproductions as well as to make corrections and some additions to the previous one.

All the photographs and quotations have been taken from the Heaven collection, except where other sources are cited. I am grateful to David Lowsley-Williams for permission to include the photograph of Cecilia Heaven; to Peter Thomas for the photograph of his grandfather, F.W. Allday; to the Lundy Field Society for photographs taken from an album made by H.W. Jukes, who was a coastguard on Lundy in 1920; and to John Dyke and Brian Le Messurier for the drawing of the Old Light.

I thank Sir John Smith for the idea that originally prompted this book, and I hope it will give as much pleasure to readers who are interested in Lundy as I have had in writing it.

Myrtle Langham (Ternstrom)
1995

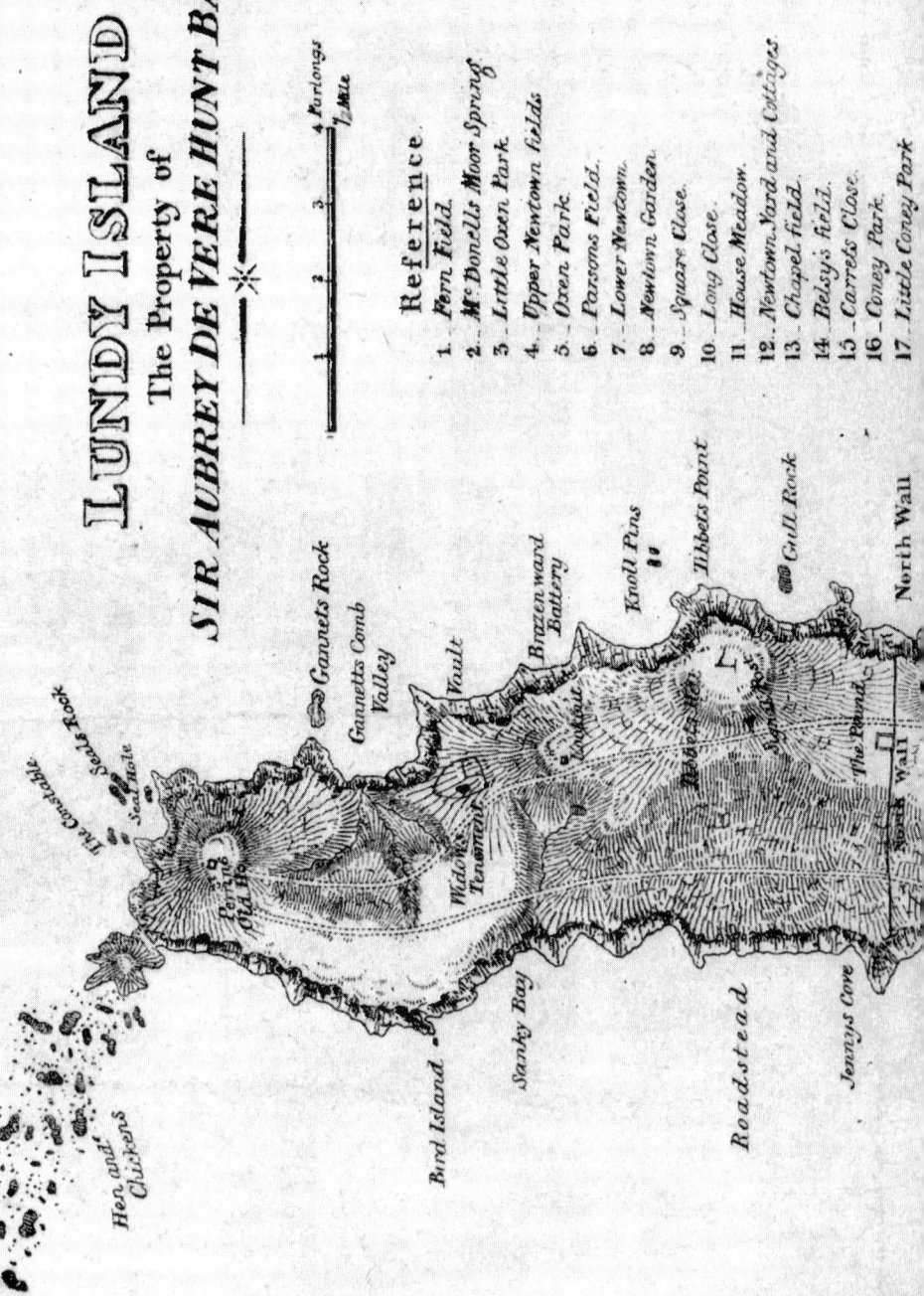

LUNDY ISLAND

The Property of
SIR AUBREY DE VERE HUNT BAR:

1   2   3   4 Furlongs
                    ½ Mile

Reference

1. Fern Field.
2. McDonells Moor Spring.
3. Little Oxen Park.
4. Upper Newtown fields.
5. Oxen Park.
6. Parsons Field.
7. Lower Newtown.
8. Newtown Garden.
9. Square Close.
10. Long Close.
11. House Meadow.
12. Newtown Yard and Cottages.
13. Chapel field.
14. Betsy's field.
15. Carrets Close.
16. Coney Park.
17. Little Coney Park

Gannets Rock
Gannetts Comb Valley
Seals Rock
The Constable
Seadrule
Hen and Chickens
Bird Island
Vault
Widows Tenement
Brazen ward Battery
Lookout
Sanky Bay
Knoll Pins
Tibbets Point
Gull Rock
Jennys Cove
Roadstead
The Pound
North Wall
South Wall

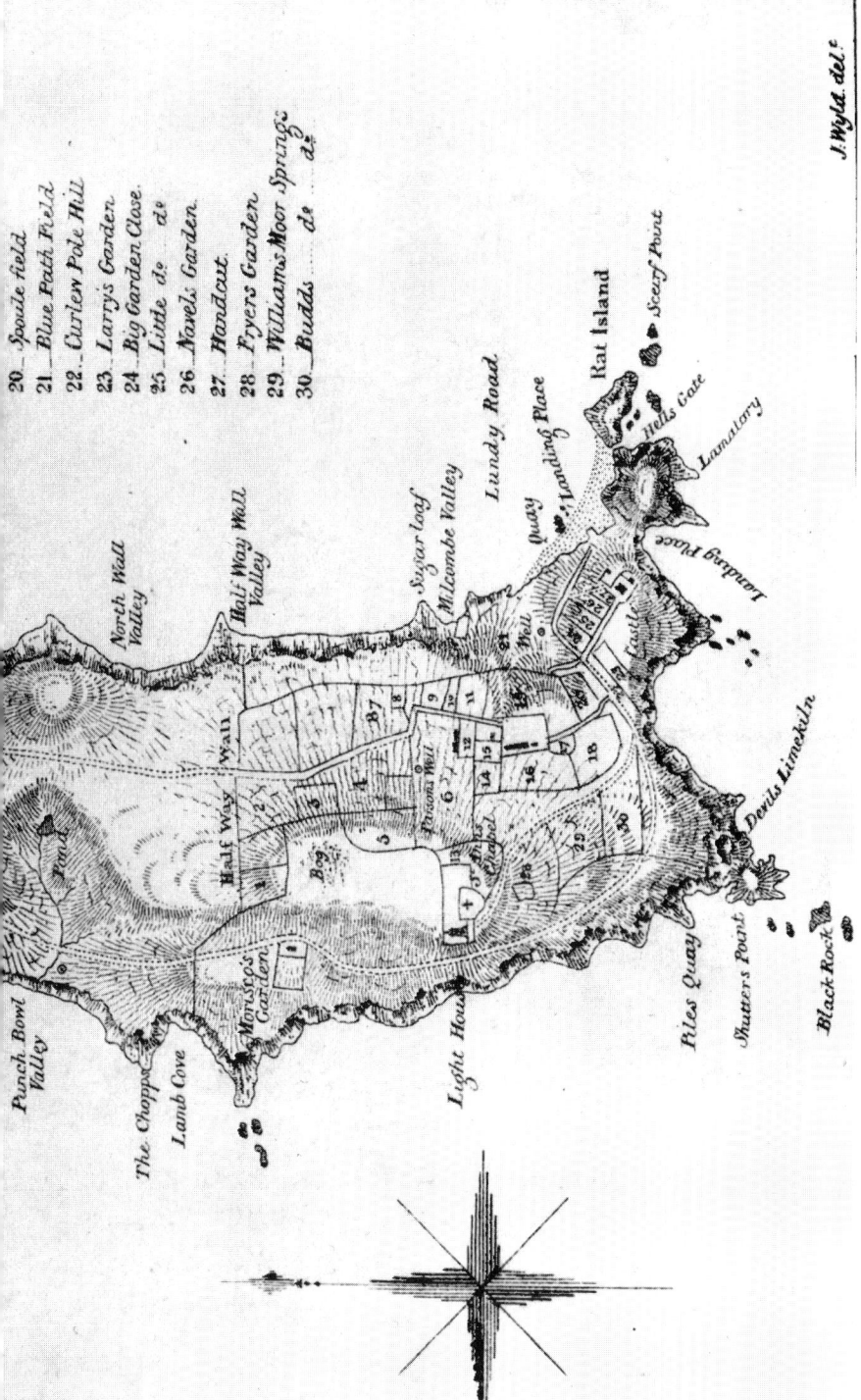

20 – Spouie field
21 – Blue Path Field
22 – Curlew Pole Hill
23 – Lary's Garden
24 – Big Garden Close
25 – Little d⁰   d⁰
26 – Novel's Garden
27 – Handcut
28 – Fryers Garden
29 – Williams Moor Springs
30 – Budds ...... d⁰ .... d⁰

Punch Bowl Valley
North Wall Valley
Half Way Wall Valley
Sugar loaf
M. Lembe Valley
Lundy Road.
Quay
Landing Place
Rat Island
Scerf Point
Halls Gate
Lametory
Landing Place
Devils Limekiln
Black Rock
Shutters Point
Ries Quay
Light House
Morisop's Garden
The Choppol
Lamb Cove
Pool
Bog
Half Way Wall
North Wall
Pisons Well
Well

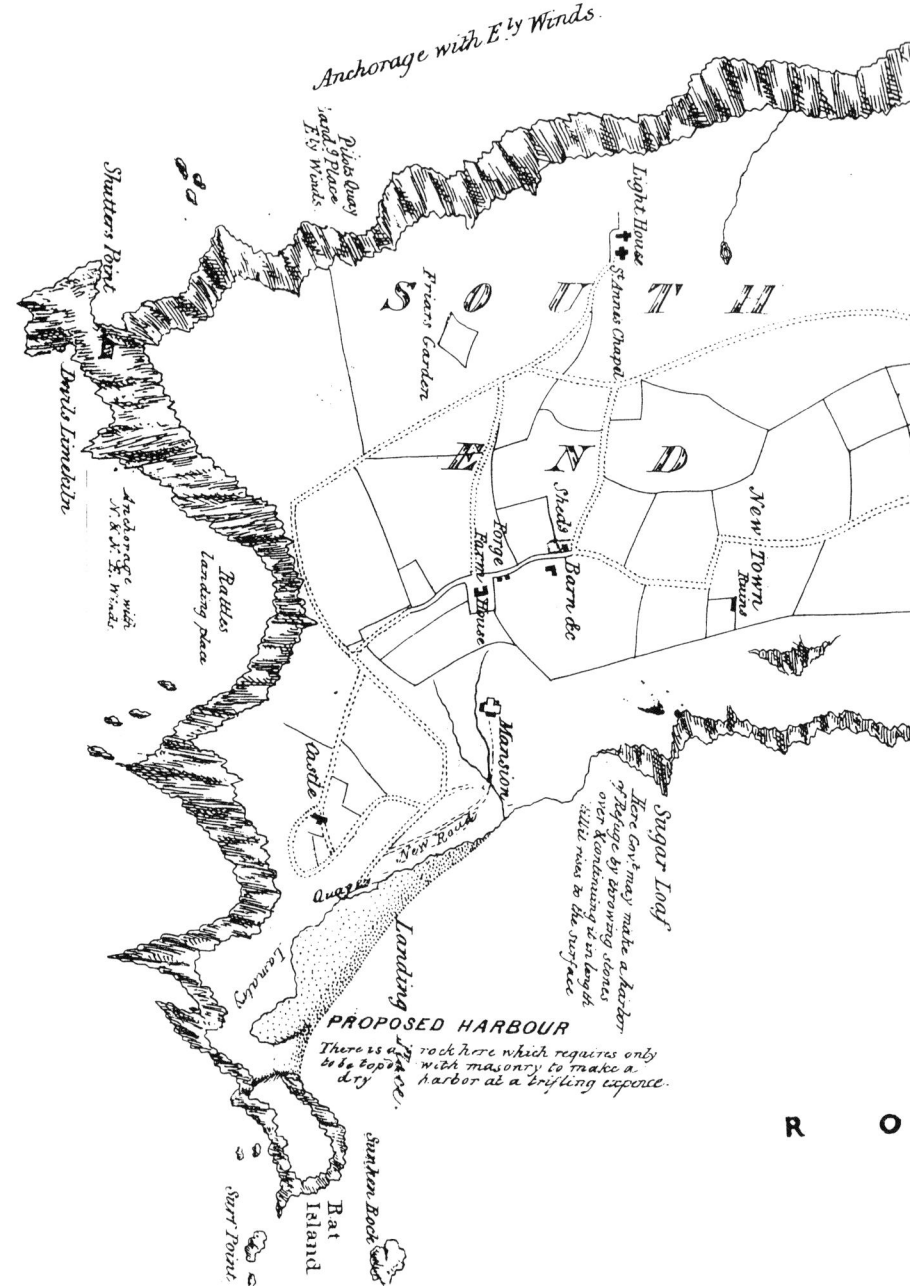

Anchorage with E.ly Winds.

Pilots Quey
and Place
E.ly Winds

Shutters Point

Devils Limekiln

Anchorage with
N.N.E. winds

Batts Landing place

SOUTH

Friars Garden

Light House
St Annas Chapel

END

Shods
Forge
Barn &c
Barn House

New Town Ruins

Castle

Mansion

Sugar Loaf

Here Gov.t may make a harbor
of Refuge by throwing stones
over Konbridging it in length
till it rises to the surface.

Quays

New Road

Landing Place

Leonards

Landing Place.

PROPOSED HARBOUR

There is a rock here which requires only
to be topped with masonry to make a
dry harbor at a trifling expence.

Sunken Rock

Surf Point

Bat
Island

R   O

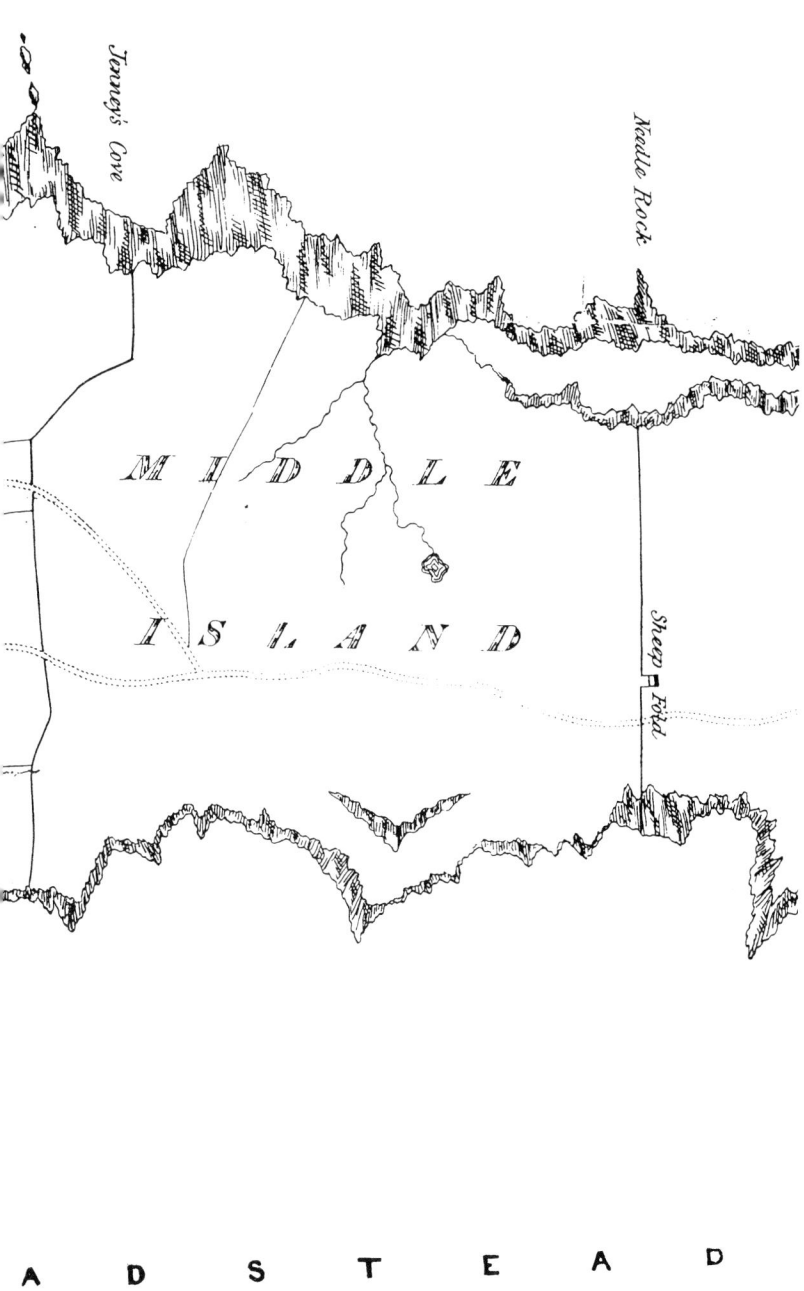

Map for the sale of the island, 1840 (south section)

The offer for sale was probably caused by the sharp decline in the price of sugar and the value of the Jamaica estates after the collapse in the price of sugar and the abolition of slavery.

William Hudson Heaven,
1832

Mrs Celia Grosett Heaven,
1832

Owners and Tenants of
LUNDY 1836–1969

1836–1883 William Hudson Heaven "The Squire"
1847–1861 Mr John Lee, tenant farmer
1862–1871 Mr W. McKenna, lessee

1883–1916 The Rev. Hudson Grosett Heaven (In Trust)
1885–1891 Mr Wright, lessee
1892–1899 Mr Ackland, lessee
1899–1908 Mr G. Taylor, lessee
1908–1912 Mr W.F. Saunt, lessee
1911–1916 Walter C.H. Heaven, tenant

1916–1917 Walter Charles Hudson Heaven

1918–1925 Augustus Langham Christie
1918–1920 Mr Dennis, Manager
1920–1925 Mr C.H. May, lessee

1925–1954 Martin Coles Harman
Agent, Mr R. Laws 1925–1926
Agent, Mr F.W. Gade 1926–1945 and 1949–1971
Agent, Mr D. Heaysman 1945–1949
Mr H. Van Os, lessee 1940–1942

1954–1968 Albion P. Harman, Ruth Harman Jones and Diana P. Keast

1968–1969 Kathleen Harman, Ruth Harman Jones and Diana P. Keast

1969 The National Trust
The Landmark Trust, lessees

The Heaven Family of Lundy

Those in **BOLD** are mentioned in the text.

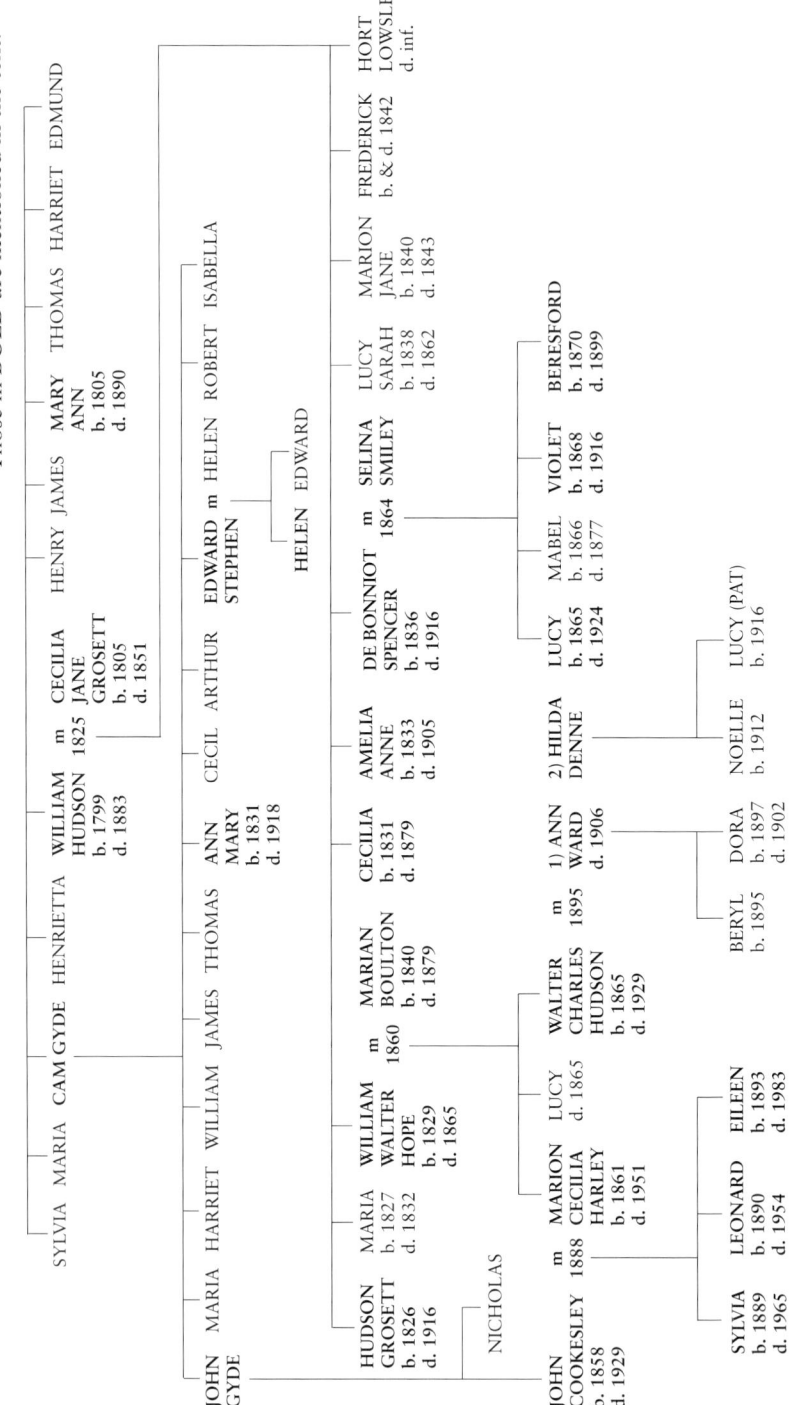

William Hudson Heaven, 1869.
Born 1799, died 1883

The son of a Gloucestershire gentleman, he was educated at Harrow and Oxford, and then made the Grand Tour with his tutor. He was heir of his godfather, William Hudson, from whom he inherited estates in Jamaica, and he was a freeman of the city of Bristol. In 1825 he married Cecilia Jane Grosett, who was noted for her beauty and sweetness of disposition, and who was the daughter of Rear-Admiral Walter Grosett. They lived at Perridge House, Pilton (near Bristol) until 1832, when they travelled with their family, and sister Mary Ann, in France.

William Hudson Heaven bought Lundy in 1836 as a summer resort for the family, and for the shooting. He appointed William Malbon as his agent on the island to supervise the farm and the building of the Villa (Millcombe); his shore agent was a Mr Chapple. After the Villa was completed, he constructed the Beach Road from the Quay to the Battlements; the materials for the Villa, and the furniture, had been hauled up the old steep track. For transport to the island in the early years he had a schoolroom yacht, *The Lady of the Isles.*

By 1842, after financial losses, and with a growing family, Mr Heaven's expense in maintaining two establishments was too great; so the greater part of the year was spent on Lundy, and a house was rented in Bristol or Clevedon for the winter. Mrs Heaven did not care to live on Lundy after the deaths of her two youngest children, when her own health was in decline, but it was the family home after her death in 1851.

In an attempt to augment his income, William Hudson Heaven leased the farm and the fishing, and explored the possibility of mining minerals; when the Granite Company leased the island, he received royalties from them on the stone exported. The leases excluded the portion of the island reserved to the owner: Millcombe, the sidelands on the east as far as Quarter Wall, the Forty-acre Field (Brick and Tillage fields), the Castle Fields, St. John's Valley and Benjamin's Chair.

William Hudson Heaven was a lay reader and a man devoted to his family. He suffered a paralytic stroke at Bristol in 1875, and when he returned to Lundy the following year he was accompanied by a doctor and a nurse as he was partially paralysed and deprived of his speech.

He had a strong concern for the rights attaching to Lundy, and defended them fiercely. He and his family were devoted to the island, and although financial troubles caused him to offer it for sale several times, neither he nor his son parted with it. He kept some title in the mainland so that he could exercise his vote without prejudice to the peculiar status of Lundy, and in 1871 he successfully challenged the right of the Court to try a case of manslaughter which had occurred on the island. Having established his point, he requested that the trial proceed, and his employee was acquitted.

Picnic at Benjamin's Chair about 1864

Left to right: William Hudson Heaven, lady unknown, the Rev. Hudson Grosett Heaven, Miss Peddar, Miss Cecilia Heaven, De Bonniot Spencer Heaven, Mrs De Bonniot Spencer Heaven (née Selina Smiley), and Miss Amelia Ann Heaven.

In summer, picnics were a much favoured diversion; note the table and benches in the background. Another selected spot was the platform on which Hanmers now stands, which also had picnic benches provided. The gentlemen were fond of shooting, and the island was stocked with woodcock, snipe, pheasants and partridges, but the most frequent bag was rabbits.

The family received many of their relatives on visits during the summer months. Among their diversions were drives, riding, walking the dogs, boating and fishing, picnics, shooting, gardening, reading, needlework, cards, visits, sewing, the piano, and reading aloud. In season there were excursions for egging, or to gather mushrooms or blackberries.

The Revd. H.G. Heaven M.A.
Born 1826, died 1916

The eldest son of William Hudson Heaven, he was educated at Oxford, took holy orders, and became a teacher. He was headmaster of Taunton College School and combined teaching with preaching in local parishes. When the school became insolvent in 1864 he returned to Lundy, and stayed to tend the spiritual needs of the population which was then enlarged by the Granite Company employees to 200–300 souls.

He was an "omnivorous reader" and as a child was nicknamed "Philosopher", which became shortened to "Phi". He was fond of shooting, walking, fishing and gardening; he occasionally took pupils, and he taught in day schools and Sunday schools for the island boys, and night school for the men. He suffered frequently from debility and minor ailments.

After his father's illness in 1875 he took charge of the island until 1885, when it was leased to a tenant (with the exception of the reserved portion). In 1885 he realised his ambition to build a church on Lundy when the iron church of St. Helen at the top of Millcombe was completed, followed by the present church of St. Helena in 1897.

In 1911 old age and ill-health forced him to leave Lundy; he went to live in Torrington but returned to the island for the summer months of 1912, 1913 and 1914. He died in 1916, and was buried on Lundy.

Millcombe, taken from Peeping Corner, Lundy, 1 August, 1838

When first built the Villa had no porch, and the outhouses and terrace were also later additions. The house had been completed in April of 1838, but the architect's report was highly critical of the joinery, plumbing, decorations and bell hangings, and stated that the composition roof was unsatisfactory. Mr Malbon had trouble with his workmen, and in obtaining materials of the required quality, which had to be sent over from the mainland. The architect who reported was Mr Edwin Honeychurch, of Bristol. It is notable that water closet apparatus was installed; the house also had wash hand-basins in the bedrooms.

The drawings were made by Mary Ann Heaven, sister to W.H. Heaven.

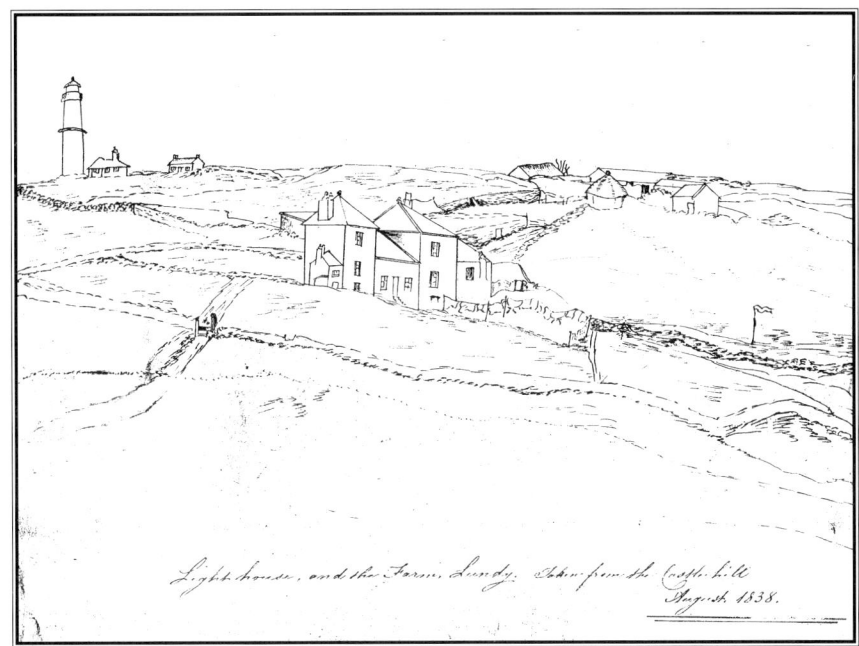

Lighthouse and Farm, Lundy, taken from Castle Hill, August 1838

The earliest picture known, this shows the house and the farm buildings as they were at the outset of the Heaven ownership. It is supposed that this is the house referred to in the account of a visit to Lundy made by a gentleman in July 1787: "You ascend into the island by a narrow path, just wide enough for a horse to get up, which leads you to a platform where two roads meet: one conducts you to the Castle (anciently Morisco's) the other (to the HOUSE lately built by Sir John Borlase Warren) wide enough for carts, and where they land goods that are to be carried off, or brought on the island."* Sir John Borlase Warren owned the island from 1777 to 1781.

At the time this drawing was made the Beach Road was under construction. Early in his ownership, Mr Heaven made alterations to the farm house by removing the pitched roofs, building up the central section, and re-building the roof with a pediment. The small cottage at the south end of the building was presumably demolished when the Quarry Company built their extension about 1868. The round structure is a hayrick; it is not possible to identify the other buildings with certainty. The Lighthouse had been constructed in 1819, and Stoneycroft is clearly shown.

* *North Devon Magazine*, Barnstaple 1824

Amelia Heaven ("Millie").
Born 1833, died 1905

The Heaven family diaries were kept from 1870 to 1905 and Millie was the main contributor throughout. Her entries are marked by occasional ironic wit and inventiveness of language (for example, a butterfly was "frivolling about").

Despite a delicate constitution she had a lively humour, and seems to have been a particular favourite among family and friends. She wrote articles and stories, based on Lundy, which were published in domestic magazines. She was well-read and knew French, German and Italian, which were useful in communicating with the crews of foreign ships that put into the Bay. She was artistic and played the piano well, and she was fond of riding. She taught the island children in both day and Sunday schools, and managed the household after her sister's death. Life on Lundy was relieved by visits to relations and friends, and receiving them as guests during the spring, summer and autumn. Her poor health caused her to break her engagement, and she never married.

She survived the amputation of one arm in her old age and kept up her correspondence to within a few days of her death. No diaries were kept after 1905.

The following extracts from her entries in the diaries indicate both her wit and the occasional languor of the family life: "Skiff came . . . skirmish as usual and every round thing in every square thing's place" . . . "Fog like a naked feather bed . . ." . . . "Everyone did nothing in particular and the rest looked on . . ." . . . "Nobody doing nothing and no-one helping.".

Her notes about the nature of the wind were something of a family joke; on 1.5.1901 she wrote, "Wind ESE and E and then perpendicular".

Cecilia was still a young woman when her mother died and she took over management of the household; she is referred to as a "born nurse" and a second mother to her niece and nephew. She was a needlewoman and a pianist, and also an occasional contributor to the diary. She became an invalid after she developed blood poisoning, and released her fiancé from an engagement that had lasted almost twenty years. She died in 1879 in the waiting-room of Barnstaple station, when she was on her way to consult a doctor, and she was buried in Bristol to spare her invalid father the news of her death.

Cecilia Heaven (Sissie).
Born 1831, died 1879
Photo: David Lowsley Williams

Violet Heaven. Born 1868, died 1916

Violet Heaven was the third child and second surviving daughter of De Bonniot Spencer Heaven and his wife, Selina, who lived at the family estate of Ramble, in Jamaica. When of school age the children returned to relatives in England, and eventually the family settled in a house called *Combe Cot* at Abbotsham. Violet was 'a gently loving soul', though nevertheless given to speaking her mind. She showed artistic talent and studied drawing in London and Paris. She visited Lundy frequently for summer holidays.

The dining-room at the Villa

The painting above the fireplace shows Mr William Hudson with his brother, James, and a negro slave. Mr Hudson left his Jamaica estates to his godson, William Hudson Heaven, and these originally consisted of 'The Ramble', 'Golden Grove', 'Silver Grove', 'Providence', 'Friendship', and 'Prosper Pens'. These were gradually sold off until only 'The Ramble' remained – 'Golden Grove' was sold about 1895 to Charles Treleven, who went to Jamaica as a clerk after he had been acquitted of intentionally shooting a drunken seaman on Lundy in 1871.

Mrs Walter Heaven (née Marian Boulton). Born 1840, died 1879

William Walter Hope Heaven (Walter).
Born 1829, died 1865

The second son of William Hudson Heaven was educated at Oxford and went to Australia in 1853 at the time of the gold fever. He found some gold, but was robbed of it, so settled in Sydney where he worked firstly in the Crown Land Office, and then as a teacher in a grammar school. In 1860 he married Marian Boulton and they had three children, but he succumbed to liver disease in 1865.

Mrs Marian Heaven, son and daughter, 1866

Marian Boulton was born in Somerset and went to Australia, with her family, as a child. The little girl is Marion Cecilia Harley (born 1861), and the baby is Walter Charles Hudson Heaven. During 1865 her second daughter, Lucy, died of scarlet fever and Marion was seriously ill; on November 17th Walter was born, and sixteen days later his father died. Early in 1866 Mrs Heaven set sail for England with the two children to live with her husband's family, whom she had never met.

She was an attractive and lively woman, who became fond of her relations, but was always conscious of her dependence on them. She was a very capable and practical person, a good needlewoman, and able to sew upholstery and hang wallpaper. She died suddenly of heart failure at the early age of 39, when she had crossed to Bristol to visit her daughter who was at school there.

He was the third son of William Hudson Heaven. He entered service with P & O, and subsequently went out to Jamaica to manage his father's estates there, returning to spend holidays with the family on Lundy. In 1864 he married Selina Smiley and they had four children of whom the third daughter, Violet, was an artist of some talent. When his health gave way in the West Indian climate, Spencer returned to England and left as estate manager his son, Beresford, who unfortunately died of fever in 1899 at the age of 29. The Jamaica estate passed to his daughter, Lucy, then to his great-nephew, Leonard Gyde Hudson Heaven.

*De Bonniot Spencer Heaven
(Spencer). Born 1836, died 1916*

A nephew of William Hudson Heaven, and brother to Ann Mary. He went to sea, but suffered from tuberculosis and was invited to stay at Lundy for the benefit of his health. Unfortunately he succumbed to this illness, died on Lundy, and was buried there.

Mr Heaven's widow and children were assisted by their relatives, and the two children, Helen and Edward, were the particular care of Ann Mary. In 1905 Helen went to live on Lundy in order to care for her aunt and uncle, and she moved to Torrington with them in 1911. Until the Great War they all returned to Lundy each year for the summer months.

*Edward Stephen Heaven.
Born 1837, died 1883*

When it was necessary to summon a doctor to the island urgently to attend this Mr Heaven, it is recorded that if a boat was needed, one fire was lit on Beacon Hill; if a doctor was needed, two fires were lit.

A younger sister of William Hudson, Miss Heaven copied down the family history from her aunt, and made the drawings of Lundy in 1838 which appear in this book. She made her home with her sister and two brothers, staying with each in turn; after her brother, Cam Gyde Heaven, died she spent the winters with her sister, and the summers on Lundy. Both households had "Aunt Mary Ann's room". After William Hudson Heaven died she went to Lundy only once, as the journey became too much for her. "A clever woman . . . she had the gift of interesting children . . was very animated".

Mary Ann Heaven.
Born 1805, died 1890

Ann Mary Heaven ("Cousin Annie").
Born 1831, died 1918

She was a niece of William Hudson Heaven. When her grandmother died in 1871, he offered Ann Mary a home at Lundy; she arrived with all her effects in 1873, and stayed until she moved to Torrington with her cousin, the Rev. Hudson Heaven, in 1911.

She was a spirited, rather forthright person who was fond of outdoor life and, with her dogs, she would accompany her cousin or the farm manager about the island when they were shooting, fishing, salving wreckage, or tending the cattle and sheep. She was also fond of gardening. She could be kind and generous, but lacked tact, and she resented any invasion of the privacy of the estate.

The Beach about 1864

Left to right: Mrs De Bonniot Spencer Heaven, De Bonniot Spencer Heaven, Amelia
Ann Heaven, Cecilia Harriet Heaven (Sissy), Miss Peddar, and Mr Harry St. John. Mr
St. John was a keen photographer.

Messing about on the beach is referred to in the family diaries as "scurrifunging".
   This photograph was taken before the Quarry Cottages were built, and there is no
evidence of the Quarry workings.
   Not infrequent resort was made to Rattles Landing Place, The Gates, and Pilot's
Quay when weather conditions made use of the landing bay impossible. Pilot's Quay
has fallen away since then.

The Beach before 1892

The Limekiln can be seen behind the boat on the Quay. The quay was either built by Sir John Borlase Warren or he rebuilt one made by Sir Bevill Grenvile in 1631. There is a slip to the beach which is shorter and steeper than the present one, and there is a large rock where the modern slipway is. The rock is probably the one called "Little Lundy" which was blown up in 1892 to make way for the extension of the slipway. The position of the horses suggests that the end of the path was steep; in 1838 William Malbon lamented "the road to the Quay which we were obliged to make every tide". There are many references in the diaries to landslips on the Beach Road, and also references to workmen carrying out "pitching" (laying with stones).

It is interesting to speculate whether some kind of direct route from the Beach to the Castle was used in earlier times. The writer of the 1752 account of a visit to Lundy says "The path . . . was so narrow and steep, that it was scarcely possible for a horse to ascend it. The inhabitants, by the assistance of a rope, climbed up a rock, in which were steps cut out to place their feet, up to a Cave . . . where Mr Benson lodged his goods . . .".[1] When Mr Gade first went to Lundy in 1926 he was told by Bob Helson that he had crossed to Lamatry by means of wooden steps below Benson's Cave, although Mrs Allday Thomas – who lived on Lundy from 1896 to 1906 – denied this.

[1] *North Devon Magazine*, Barnstaple 1824

A Slipway about 1864

Left to right: De Bonniot Spencer Heaven, Mr G. Maule, the Rev. Hudson Grosett Heaven and Tom Lee. Mr Maule was a family friend who made frequent visits to the island from Ilfracombe, where he lived at No. 1, Hillsborough Terrace; he was a barrister, and had a yacht called *Foam*. Tom Lee was a Trinity House employee living at the Battery. It is clear from the Heaven family diaries that Trinity House men joined in the general work about the island; it is recorded that Tom Lee was in trouble for poaching and that his gun was confiscated. He left the island in 1873 after a protest had been made to Trinity House.

This shows the old narrow, short slipway which ended in steps. The extension was built by Trinity House in 1892. A description of hauling loads in 1871 notes that:

"*The smack with coal came the next day, on her beaching, all the men were busy unloading her till tide flowed again. There was no slip extension then: it ended in steep, roughly hewn steps in the trap-dyke by the present steps leading over the shale to Lamatry. Planks were placed from Slip to Beach over the steps to form a gangway, built up by shingle over furze bushes, and the horses drew sleds of coal in sacks to the Quay, or if there was time, the gangway was enlarged to allow a cart to be driven down and up again when loaded*".

The Fish Palace, 1874

The island fishing was rented by men from Sennen, and the rental of £10.00 p.a. included the use of this building. The door, which can be seen here, led into a large room which had a store-room below it; the lobster pots can be seen to the left of the picture, with the net poles. The building, or an earlier version of it, is shown in the painting by Dominic de Serres of 1775.

Lobster, crayfish and crabs were caught and sold in the season, and in autumn large numbers of mackerel and herring were caught, as many as 400 or more being recorded in a single catch. When there was a glut, fish was salted so long as the salt held out; sometimes they were smoked, and a diary entry for 1894 reads, "(Mr) Dear smoking herrings in the powder-proof place by Benson's Cave."

Catches were sold on the mainland; either Captain Dark came over on a tide suitable to take the fish back to market, or the fishermen took it across to the mainland themselves in their own boat.

Other kinds of fish were caught occasionally and attempts were made to harvest conger and mullet. Variety of fish for the table was more often obtained from the many boats which used the Bay for shelter, to replenish supplies, or to obtain assistance of some kind.

Old and New Beach Roads

Before William Hudson Heaven built the new Beach Road from the Quay to "Peeping Corner" in 1838 it was not possible to use carts for haulage from the beach. "Everything was carried on ponies or donkeys, or on sleds." Mrs Heaven continues: "William Hudson Heaven . . . considering the strain of dragging supplies too much for man and beast up the old road, approached the Elder Brethren of Trinity House to collaborate in making the new road . . . they had to supply engineers and (skilled) labour and to divide the cost between them, the haulage of T.H. stores, coal and oil etc. being by far the heaviest usage of the road. Their advisory engineers being of the opinion the said proposed road was practically impossible, W.H.H. was his own engineer, and had it constructed, but on the Elder Brethren wanting to use it, he refused to permit its use, restricting them to their legal right of way, and later an agreement was arranged, so that it should be (used and) kept in repair by Trinity House . . . The 'Battlements' were built by W.H.H. . . . there being some danger of falling over the edge in trying to turn that corner when going down the road beyond a walking pace" with horse and cart. The white cottage at the point where the old and new roads converged was used by the fishermen who came to Lundy for the season, and was named "Sea View". It was furnished and had a stove. The hut at the bottom of the path was a store.

The Beach Road before 1896

The *Prince of Wales* was the regular excursion boat during the summer months of the 1870s; later the *Velindra* and the *Brighton* were employed, coming on Tuesdays and Fridays when the weather permitted.

The organisers of excursions were required to obtain permission to land, but when this was not forthcoming they did not always desist from coming, and the "scursioners" were not welcome to the family. No landing fees were taken until Mr Taylor made this charge when he was lessee.

Horses and carts and donkeys were used for haulage; heavy loads were beached, and it sometimes took several days to transport them to the top of the island.

The coal always came in a special boat and it was necessary to mobilise all the available manpower and horse-power to haul it from the Beach. The Lighthouse men helped when not on duty, and men were borrowed from the estate or from the farm, as the case may be; the loads for the tenant and for the Heaven family were brought separately. Employees were 'loaned' at hay-making time and on other occasions when necessary during those periods when the farm was let to tenants.

There seems to be a path up to Lamatry – there is reference to a path "over Lamatry" and samphire was collected there regularly.

The Velindra *excursion steamer about 1890*

This photograph shows the *Velindra* which called regularly at this time with Capt. Pocket. Visitors also came to the island in the *Gannet*, in private yachts, and in small vessels which could be hired from neighbouring ports. Objection was made to excursion parties which were of a rowdy or ill-conducted nature, and the gates to the Villa were firmly closed to trespassers.

Visitors of appropriate social standing would send cards up to the Squire, or make a formal call and ask permission to see the island. If they claimed connection with the family or friends, they would be given a tour and possibly entertained to lunch or tea. Gifts of fresh fruit and newspapers were much appreciated, and were reciprocated with gifts of island produce. Visitors' offering to take mail away was a courtesy always appreciated and, prior to the installation of the telegraph, the correct time and the latest news were both obtained from visiting ships.

Visitors who became stranded were fed and accommodated as suited their status: working people were allowed the Castle cottages or billeted with an islander; gentlefolk were accorded the use of the Quarry cottages or boarded at the farm; ladies and gentlemen of standing were entertained at the Villa if there was room.

The Common before 1872

The present battlemented boundary wall was commenced in 1872. That the photograph was taken before 1894 is established from the absence of the Rocket Life-Saving Apparatus hut which was built to the south of the Barn in that year.

On the extreme left of this photograph the path continues westwards to the Lighthouse; it skirted the Tent Field, and in several places evidence of the made-up path can still be seen. The Lighthouse was supplied with stores by the *Chance* of Clovelly, which called twice each month, and by Trinity House vessels which came annually. The goods were hauled up from the beach, or else landed at Pilot's Quay if conditions were unsuitable in the Bay. Thus, this path would have been in regular use by the horses and carts necessary to supply the Lighthouse.

This photograph offers an interesting comparison with the drawing of 1838.

The Village between 1885 and 1894

The Schoolhouse was built in 1886, but from the diaries it seems that it was principally a Sunday school, as weekday afternoon and evening lessons were given at "The House". The Revd. Mr Heaven taught the boys, and "Miss Annie" (Ann Mary Heaven) taught the girls and infants, assisted by Millie, Marian or Winnie when needed. The Schoolhouse here has no kitchen extension, which must have been added after the Heaven family sold the island and the building was brought into use for residence. It was used for letting, or for staff, until in 1976 it was refurbished and the kitchen extension rebuilt to make it suitable for holiday lettings. The building to the south of it, which now forms the central section of the St. John's Cottages, was a shed and stable. As it is in the reserved portion of the island, the hay mow presumably belonged to the Heaven family, as did the cultivated gardens in St. John's Valley itself.

The Barton cottages are seen with their original pitched roofs; there were eight cottages, which had upstairs rooms, and at one time a donkey was kept under the stairs of one of the cottages! These cottages were built between 1861 and 1871, which most probably means that they were built by the Granite Company. Originally they were called "Sea View".

Millcombe between 1872 and 1885

The Heaven family called their residence "The Villa", but in the latter part of their ownership it was more commonly referred to as "The House". It was not known as "Millcombe" until Mr M.C. Harman became owner.

The house was completed in 1838 after many trials and tribulations, not least of which was the necessity of hauling eveything that was required for the work up the old steep path from the Beach, using horse-drawn sleds. The agent, William Malbon, had trouble from his workmen and trouble in obtaining everything that he required from the mainland; when the Villa was finished he considered it unsatisfactory in the workmanship, and caused an architect's report to be made before the accounts were settled.

The porch, terrace, and outhouses were later additions. Of the outhouses, the carriage shed can just be seen on the far right, next to what was the harness room, then two laundry rooms (here with steaming chimney) and a gun room. The outside W.C. against the north face of the house was removed during Mr Harman's ownership. In this photograph two windows appear which are now blanks (the centre window above the porch and the first floor window on the north face). Probably these two are false, as in none of the photographs are they seen open, and there are no signs of windows inside.

The white fencing behind the house was to mark the path up to the farm (1878), and the wall dividing Millcombe from the Farmhouse lawn was called the Boundary Wall.

At the end of the terrace is the "House Beautiful", which was an outside shelter for Miss Amelia Heaven, who was in delicate health. The comment that it was unsightly caused her to protest that "It is the house beautiful. That is the ugly one up there!" whereupon "The Ugly" received its name; the knoll is most often referred to as "Heath Mount" in diaries and letters.

Millcombe about 1890–1900

"Lodore"

The Heaven family were keen gardeners, and a wide variety of plants was grown, especially flowering shrubs. The gardens were fully cultivated as it was necessary to be as self-sufficient as possible; in addition to the usual kitchen produce, it is recorded that at least one fig was produced on the fig tree, and melons and strawberries were harvested, as well as good crops of apples. A bee garden was kept and honey produced. Also chickens, ducks, turkeys, pigs and cows were kept.

There was housing for the carts in the stable at the bottom of the drive. When the site was being cleared for this building, human remains were uncovered, and care was taken not to cause further disturbance.

The container for the waterfall was built in 1870, and the name of this place was "Lodore". The porch of the Villa had been renewed in 1879, and the stucco replaced in 1890.

Tea in the hall, about 1900

The children are Sylvia, Leonard and Eileen Heaven.

The hall was used as an extra sitting-room, and the porch as a miniature conservatory. The inhabitants of the house at this time were the Revd. Hudson Heaven, Miss Amelia Heaven and Miss Ann Mary Heaven. They had a cook, a housemaid, a parlourmaid, a laundrymaid and a groom-gardener when there were no staff problems; in times of difficulty the wives and children of the islanders were recruited to help.

The hall at the Villa

The painting, by Monanteuil, is of the four children of William Hudson Heaven in 1832; from the left are Hudson Grosett, Maria Ann (died soon after this portrait was painted), William Walter Hope, and Cecilia Harriet. This picture now hangs above the staircase and was given to the Landmark Trust by Miss Eileen Heaven.

The drawing-room at the Villa about 1874

Living in the house at this time were William Hudson Heaven ("The Squire"), Hudson Grosett Heaven, Amelia and Cecilia Heaven, Mrs Marian Heaven and her two children, and Ann Mary Heaven; there were also a cook and three maids.

Every year a Christmas supper was given for the workmen and their wives, when the family plate, "good china" and candles were used, and the family all donned festive raiment and jewels for the occasion. After supper the men were allowed to smoke in the laundry while the women cleared away; then followed games in the hall, picture books in the drawing-room, charades, and dancing (to piano). The children were given a separate party of their own a few days later. Each year there was a Christmas tree in the dining-room; all the islanders came down on the evening before Christmas to receive their presents, except the children who were given theirs after church on Christmas morning.

The only times that the islanders came to the house otherwise were for Sunday services or when they borrowed from the 1,200 or more books, or came for remedies, help and advice. There is a reference in the diaries to a "Physic room". The family kept a supply of medicines and the Revd. Heaven became particularly skilled in First Aid. When the patient was in need of a doctor's care either the doctor was sent for from Ilfracombe or Instow, or the patient was taken to the mainland if he or she was in a condition to withstand the journey.

The drawing-room after 1889

The fireplace has been tiled, a new overmantel and new furniture installed.

The carriage with Mr Ward in attendance, about 1890

The Heaven ladies used the carriage for excursions around the island and to the Beach, but it not infrequently came to grief on unseen boulders.

The upstairs landing at the Villa (Millcombe) about 1900–1914

The room on the right was not then a bathroom, but was called "the small room" and was used for the cook.

The door on the left was Amelia Heaven's room and the room next to it was Hudson Heaven's. The south-west room was "the Dimity Room", next to that was the maids' bedroom (for three) and the back room next to the W.C. was the Pink Room. The large front room was the Blue Room, and had been occupied by William Hudson Heaven, whose nurse occupied the small adjoining room. After his death the connecting door was replaced by a cupboard, and a large bath was installed in the small room, though a hip bath was also used; when visitors outnumbered the bedrooms, planks were put over the bath and used to sleep on.

For their time, the bedrooms were unusual in having handbasins fixed, and these were of blue and white decorated china. Miss Heaven said that they were removed to Tapely Park by Lady Christie.

Tennis on the lawn, 1888

The tennis lawn was set up in 1886 and was used by Mr Wright's family and his guests, who included the Heaven family. The gardener in the foreground is Mr Brimacombe, whose wife is standing near the store-keeper's cottage. He died in 1895 and is buried in the graveyard.

The gentleman with the horse is Mr Thomas Wright, who leased the island (with the exception of the portion reserved for the Heaven family) from 1885 to 1891. He is sometimes referred to as "Panjan"* in the diaries, which makes its own comment. He was a gentleman land agent, surveyor and farmer, fond of horses and gardens and visitors to the island were conducted to admire both.

The south wing was constructed by the Granite Company, and the interior was completed by Mr Wright for his own use as a residence. He was attended by housekeepers, one of whom, his cousin Miss Fulshaw, published an anonymous pamphlet, *The Adventures of a Visit and Scenes of Lundy Island*, 1886.

Visitors were occasionally accommodated at "the Farm" (that is, the part of the building between the south wing and the cottage) but not many or frequently. Mr Wright's successor as lessee was Mr Ackland, who went into partnership with his son-in-law, Mr Dickinson. Boarders were accommodated, and a refreshment room was put up to the west of the farmhouse where trippers were catered for. A newspaper in 1897 reported that "Those visiting the island will find every comfort. Mr Henry Ackland . . . provides excellent accommodation . . . He is storekeeper, postmaster, and everything, no-one else is allowed to trade. There is a right genial welcome for everybody . . . Mr Ackland brews beer . . ." (The newspaper cutting is not identified.)

* Panjandrum: a figure of imagined great importance

Egging

The supply of eggs was abundant, and there are several references in contemporary articles to the egg-gathering activities of the islanders which at one time had formed a considerable part of their economy. It is also clear that the taking of eggs by trespassers was very common, and that it was strongly resented.

"In May the eggs begin to be plentiful, and picking them (to use the island vernacular) occupies much of the islanders' attention . . . not only that, everybody of Lundy: depredators make forays from the mainland, and carry away their prey by boatloads, while the crews of the pilot skiffs and steam tugs seem to consider them in the light of a regular supply."*

The egg gatherer was let down the cliff by rope and collected the eggs into his shirt; he needed to be skilful in protecting both himself and his booty from jutting rocks. Obviously this operation could be hazardous, and lives were sometimes lost, as Miss Amelia Heaven describes in her fanciful little story, "Out Egging" (*After Work* Vol. 14, No. 5, 1877).

* *Social Review* 1.3.1877.

The Farm and "Big House", 1888

This photograph shows where the wall above the old doorway of the Farm was built up, and the roof raised. The single storey part (extreme right of photo) was then a washroom and there was a well under the floor. This part was not connected to the Tavern wing until 1926. To the right of the entrance steps to The Big House is a low door to an old basement dairy. The two maids are standing at the entrance to the farmhouse.

The Revd. Mr Hannington egging, 1875

The Revd. James Hannington made several visits to Lundy, and sometimes preached at the Sunday services. He wrote comic verses and made drawings about his exploits there and described how the egg-hunter armed himself with an instrument called an egg-spoon, like a tiny landing-net, at the end of a long, light rod. He was then let down over the cliff for more than twelve feet.

(He was consecrated Bishop of East Africa in 1884, where he was unfortunately put to death the following year.)

E.C. Dawson, *James Hannington*, London 1887

*Walter Charles Hudson Heaven ("Boy") Born 1865, died 1929, and his
sister Marion Cecilia Harley Heaven ("Winnie") Born 1861, died 1951.*

The children of William Walter Hope Heaven, they were born in Sydney, Australia,
and came to live on Lundy with their grandfather, uncle and aunts in 1866 after the
death of their father. Walter left Lundy in 1888 and went to Canada, Australia and
America, and returned in 1911 to take over the island after his uncle's retirement to
Torrington. On the death of the Rev. Hudson Heaven in 1916 Walter Heaven became
owner of Lundy, but he was bankrupt and was forced to sell in the following year.
His life thereafter was one of great hardship, due to unemployment; he went to
Australia with his wife and daughters, but found conditions to be as bad there as they
had been in England, both countries suffering post-war economic depression. He died
in Australia in 1929 and his ashes were brought back to Lundy for burial in 1930.

Walter Heaven had an unfortunate life. He had been brought up as gentry but had
no estate, nor education for a profession. As a boy his one passion was boats and he
wanted more than anything to go to sea, but his mother could not part with him at
the early age then necessary for that career, and after her death her relatives did not

Walter Charles Hudson Heaven

like to go against her wishes. None of Walter's various ventures in the theatre, or farming in Canada, U.S.A., England or Australia met with any success. He incurred the displeasure of all his family when he married Annie Ward, who was the daughter of the groom-gardener on Lundy. His second wife, Hilda, was much younger than he was, and after they had left Lundy became virtually destitute in Australia; they had sold all their possessions and she had to resort to the family in England to meet the expenses of sending the ashes for burial on Lundy.

Many of the photographs in this book were taken by Dr John Cookesley Heaven, to whom Winnie was married in 1888. She contributed to the history of the Heaven family, and wrote the reminiscences of her life on Lundy from which much of the information given in this book is drawn. She based those reminiscences on the diaries, but unfortunately had only completed them to 1877 before she died.

Mrs Heaven inherited her grandfather's strong attachment to Lundy, and his strong sense of family. She spent nearly all her summers there, and continued to visit the island to the end of her life, maintaining a deep interest in all that concerned it.

Her younger daughter, Miss Eileen Heaven, lent the photographs and papers which form the substance of this book.

George Thomas

George Thomas came to Lundy from Sennen each summer for the fishing, which a group of fishermen rented. After 1879 he became an island employee and lived first at the Castle, then at Quarry Cottages until, in 1898–9, he built the bungalow which is now called Hanmers. It cost him £150 and was called "The Palace". He was fisherman, boatman, handyman, and the first to be called upon in any kind of contingency; he became indispensible to the Heaven family. He and his wife, Susan, had four sons, and a daughter called "Hetty" who died tragically in 1892 when she fell over the cliff at the S.W. point and was lost without trace.

"The Palace" was originally a corrugated-iron building consisting of the three main rooms (kitchen and two bedrooms) with a wash-house extension at the back. After George Thomas left the island the Revd. W. Swatridge lived there, he drank, and once chased his wife with a carving-knife! Later the cottage was occupied by Mr & Mrs Allday, who paid £10 p.a. for it.

The house was known as "Cliff Bungalow" until the Hanmer family became regular visitors in the 1930s and it was eventually referred to as "Hanmers".

It has been remarked that the field behind Hanmers has no name. The Heaven family called it "Lower Castle Field", and the field containing Castle Hill was "Upper Castle Field". These two were included in the reserved part of the island and were used for crops and hay and for grazing. The area surrounding the Castle was known as "Castle Park".

Miss Eileen Heaven, c. 1914

Eileen Heaven was born in 1893, the youngest of three children. Her mother grew up on Lundy and was the granddaughter of William Hudson Heaven; her father was the grandson of William's brother, Cam Gyde. The family lived in Bristol where Dr John Heaven was a surgeon and agent to the Admiralty, and summer holidays were spent on Lundy. Although Eileen did particularly well at school, there was no money to further her education and she became a teacher of dancing.

At Lundy Lodge, Portishead, c. 1950. Photo: Stanley Smith

Lundy Lodge was a house with Victorian character, and was full of Lundy paintings, photographs, family china, furniture, and papers. She lived there with her mother, 'her help and confidante', until the latter's death in 1951, and then alone until forced by ill-health to move into a residential home, where she died in 1983. She had a quiet and refined manner, but was of hardy and intelligent character, with an unexpected sense of humour. She continued to visit Lundy every year so long as she was able to get there, and took a daily swim in the bay – whatever the temperature.

Her brother, Leonard, had no children. Her sister, Sylvia, had a daughter and two grandchildren, and her uncle, Walter, had three daughters who went to Australia and South Africa. These are the sole descendants of William Hudson Heaven's ten children.

The Manor House, 1888

This picture shows the south face of the "New House" after it had been completed as a residence by Mr Wright. The bay window gave a view to the east from the drawing room – this window has now been moved and gives the same view from the new Tavern. Behind the sitting room were a dining room, a sitting room, a kitchen, and a store. Lloyds, the lighthouse, the Battery, the Villa (at the Ugly), the Manor House and, later, the church all had flagstaffs where flags were raised on high days and holidays, or at half mast in mourning. The flags were hoisted when the Squire returned to the island after an absence.

Mr Wright can be seen in the garden with his dog. He discouraged unwanted excursionists by turning the bull out on to the common, with a warning notice! Chanter comments that he 'greatly extended cultivation and . . . the productive capabilities of the island, particularly for trade in livestock.'*

* *J.R. Chanter,* Lundy Island, *London 1887*

Mrs Hilda Heaven (née Denne)

Hilda Denne married Walter Heaven in 1907 when she was 18 and he was 42. For the Heaven family she was not *persona grata*, although it was admitted that she was capable, energetic and good-natured. She may have thought she was marrying a man of property, but in truth she faced a life of hard work and poverty. When they took over Lundy in 1911 the island was in a run-down state, and it was a struggle to try to make ends meet without having either capital or any other income. The outbreak of war in 1914 compounded the problems. They were their own labourers; the Villa stood empty and the family lived in the farmhouse. Two daughters were born, but not counting these or their nursemaid, the total population in 1916 was only 9, mostly elderly souls. By the end of the next year the struggle to keep Lundy was over, and it had to be put up for sale.

The family went to Australia where life was equally difficult, and Mrs Heaven had to resort to knitting for an income. She remained in Australia after the death of her husband, and in 1937 she returned to Lundy for one last visit.

St. Helen's

The Granite Company built an iron room (where the sheep dip now is in the High St.) and this fulfilled many of the functions of a parish hall. Services were held there until it was dismantled when the Granite Company left in 1871. After that services were held in "The Big House" or in the hall at the Villa. When the Revd. Mr Heaven was indisposed or away on the mainland, "Readings" were held instead of services.

The Iron Church, St. Helen's, was a pre-fabricated building which was erected in approximately eight days. It was dedicated by the Bishop of Exeter on 20 August 1885, although the interior was still incomplete. This church continued in used until the new granite church was completed in 1897, but as the land remained in private ownership it was a dedicated and not a consecrated building, so no marriages could be celebrated there. When Miss Marion Heaven was married in 1888 the banns were called at Hartland (the nearest parish church) and the ceremony took place at Bristol.

The interior of the iron church of St. Helen looks surprisingly spacious

It could seat about 60 people, and there is record of at least one occasion when there was not enough room – this was when the island congregation was augmented by the crews of ships anchored in the bay.

Services were held regularly after the Revd. Mr Heaven returned to live on Lundy in 1864. There was "practice" every Saturday evening, two services on the first Sunday in each month and one on other Sundays, as well as on all days of religious observance. Visiting clergy were invited to preach, and when relatives were staying on the island they usually read the lessons, while one of the ladies of the family played the harmonium (which can be seen on the right of the picture above). After the new church was built, the iron church was used as a parish room and was referred to as the "Mission Room". The small pond nearby was called 'The quarry pool'.

Old Quarry Cottages, 1905

These were built by the Granite Company for their officers: the north cottage was used by Mr Gray, the Clerk of Works; the centre cottage by Mr Kyle, the manager; and the south cottage by the doctor (firstly Dr Linacre, then Dr Snow).

After the Granite Company left the island, the Heaven family refurbished the cottages in 1872 for the use of visiting relatives and friends. They were also let to selected tenants for holidays, or for the shooting; the rent of a cottage was £24 per annum, and the rent of the shooting £30 per annum. At that time they were known as "Belle Vue", or "North, Mid & South Cottages". "Quarter Wall Cottages" was the name given to the houses near the main track at Quarter Wall, originally called "North Row" and "South Row", which were dismantled to provide stone for buildings elsewhere, some being used for the Signal Cottages and St Helena's Church.

The Old Quarry Cottages shown here continued in use for many years, and the south cottage was not abandoned until 1921. The nearby Quarry with the pool is referred to as "William Heard's Quarry"; it is recorded that a wooden bridge across to the time office collapsed in 1890.

The Quarries were always referred to as "The Works". Unfortunately the existing diaries date only from 1870, when the Granite Company had ceased operations, so there are no descriptions of this interesting venture.

Concert party, 13 October 1886. Illustration: Vanity Fair, *1886*

This was held in the newly-built Schoolroom, and the harmonium was moved from the church for the occasion. Most of the islanders were present, and the concert was judged to be a great success. The artist recording the event, Miss Violet Heaven, is sitting at bottom right of the picture. At this time concert parties were held frequently, usually "behind the Store", and probably because Walter Heaven was an enthusiast.

The Gannet

Captain Dark of the *Gannet* always carried the mail for the Heaven family in their own box, which was delivered to and collected from the Villa. At times when the skiff had been delayed, odd letters were frequently carried by visitors and islanders travelling by any other vessel; this was a courtesy that was much appreciated, as was the receipt of newspapers. Until 1897 the Lighthouse also had its own letter box, which was conveyed by Captain Cox (in the *Chance* from Clovelly) who had the Trinity House contract. Thus, for some years there were, with the G.P.O., three distinct mail systems in existence concurrently.

Mr & Mrs Ward at the Bungalow

The Wards came to Lundy in 1877, living first at the Quarter Wall cottages, and staying until the Revd. Mr Heaven retired to the mainland in 1911. He was groom/gardener/coachman and she was a cook. They had five children; the eldest son, Fred, was storekeeper about 1884–5 and "an attractive Don Juan" who was dismissed from the island when one of the maids became pregnant. The youngest child, Annie, went to Australia with her brother, John, and Walter Heaven, who married her there in 1895.

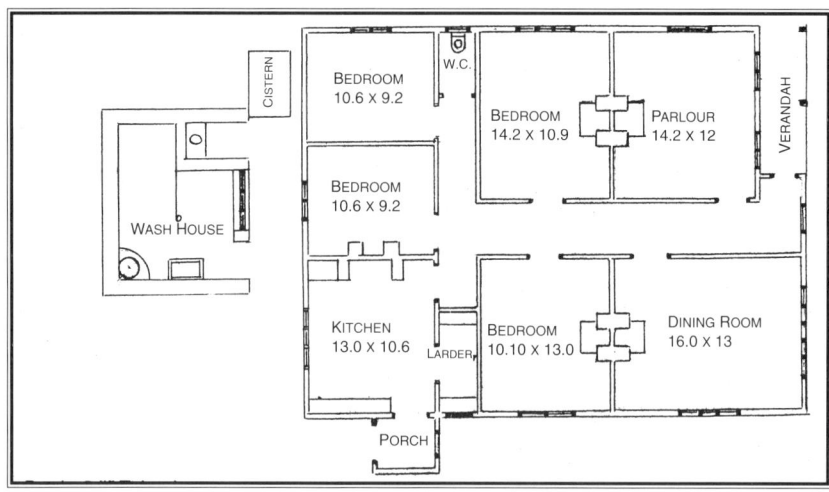

The Bungalow plan (1918)

Reproduced by permission of the North Devon Record Office. Ref: B170 add/39/52

The Bungalow

This corrugated iron house was built in 1892–93 by contractors who were assisted by island labour. It was divided in use: Mr and Mrs Ward occupied one bedroom, a sitting room and the kitchen; the rest was reserved for the use of the Heaven family as an extension to "the House". Miss Eileen Heaven said that when her family spent the summer holidays on Lundy the children, with their nurse, were accommodated in the Bungalow, and that "Uncle Phi" used the dining room as a study. The children did not have their meals at "The House" unless they were invited.

The Bungalow continued to be used for staff accommodation or for letting until 1970, when it was dismantled and a new house erected on the site. In modern times the Bungalow, and the house which succeeded it, have been called "Brambles".

The Store

This was first established by the Granite Company (1863–1868) and when they left the islanders petitioned Mr Heaven to retain it, which he did. He had the premises cleaned, took stock, and a Mr Gooding arrived in 1871 to take charge. He was succeeded in 1873 by a Mr Pullen.

The lessees were responsible for the store after 1885. Mr Ackland took the Store over from Mr Wright in 1891, before he took the farm lease, and he appointed a Mr Wainford to be in charge of it and act as postmaster.

The older of these two photographs dates from 1885, when Mr Frederick Ward was storekeeper. It shows the building with two doors and two windows, and the notice simply says "Store".

Mr Pennington second from right

The second photo was taken about 1906 when Mr William Pennington was storeman. The notice above the door reads: "Stores Provisions and Refreshments" and it is possible that Mr Ackland may have ex-tended or re-organised the Store.

Interior of the Store, July 1906
Mr Pennington is at the bar. Photo from the *Wide World Magazine.*

Mr A.J. Dennis in *Lundy Review* No. 5 says that in 1917 the Store was an oil store, and that parties were held in the Manor House kitchen. Mrs Phyllis Squire (née Blackburn, a relative of Mr Herbert May) says that there was a bar in the Store in 1920 but it was known as "The Canteen".

The description in 1906 makes it plain that the Store was also the pub: *"The photograph shows the only shop, or store, at which any purchase can be made. It has the distinction, also, of being the only inn in the British Isles that requires no licence, and it is open at any hour of the day or night . . . The Store . . . is very like the sort of thing one would expect to see in the Klondyke; it is the only place where one can buy food."*

In the later photograph one of the doorways has been replaced by a window, which suggests that possibly two rooms may have been converted to one. In *Lundy Review* No. 4 reference is made to a George IV penny having been found during work to a bar window in 1954. The part of the building at the west end was the Bakehouse, of which the oven remains in the south wall.

A picnic on the occasion of Queen Victoria's Jubilee, 1897

On 20 June a special commemoration service was held in the new church, which had been consecrated by the Bishop of Exeter three days earlier. On the 22nd the *Brighton* pleasure steamer wired that it was not coming and "the lunch prepared therefore by Mr Ackland for the 'scursion' was turned into a Jubilee feast . . . followed by sports at which everyone but Annie & Millie assisted."

Bellringers, 21 September 1898

Back row: G. Bowen, the Revd. Martin, the Revd. H.G. Heaven, the Revd. H. Pigot, W. Vickery, F. Reed.
Front row: J. German, W. Carnell, W. Slocombe, R. Dadds, A. Dadds.

The Ilfracombe Band of Change Ringers arrived on the *Lady Margaret*. The Revd. Mr Heaven entertained the two clergymen to lunch at the Villa, while the men were given lunch "at the tent". What was rung is not recorded, but this must have been the occasion when the bells were first rung by a team of ringers.

The second was on 23 August 1905 when change ringers from the Gloucester & Bristol Diocesan Assn. rang a Steadman peal of 5040 changes in 2 hours 53 minutes. Before they could do this, they had to carry out some repairs. This time the whole party was given lunch at the Villa.

Lighthouse keepers with their families, 1893

From the left: Mr Hast, R. McCarthy, Capt. Reed of a pleasure steamer, Mr McCarthy (principal keeper), Lily Hast, ?Miss Hall, Mr Hall with ?Lilian McCarthy and his son, unknown, Augustus McCarthy, ?Louise McCarthy, Mrs McCarthy, the photographer's daughter, Janie McCarthy.

Mrs Hast died suddenly in August 1892 and is buried in the graveyard. There had been much illness at the lighthouse in those years, and it was found that the water supply was contaminated by waste.

Mr McCarthy was appointed in 1884 and left in 1893. In 1892 he was awarded a testimonial by the R.N.L.I. for his "gallant and successful exertions" in the rescue of the crew of 21 from the *Tunisie*. The rescue took place in a blinding snowstorm and lasted for seven hours. For the same rescue George Thomas was awarded a medal by the Board of Trade, and the ten other rescuers received £3 each – these included Mr Hall, Mr Hast, Mr Ackland and Mr Ward. George Thomas commented that the medal was very nice but, for a working man, "the money would have been more useful".*

Mr McCarthy had seven sons and daughters, and all the lighthouse children received their education from the Heaven family. The island children went down to the Villa every Christmas morning and were each given the present of a book.

*B. Le Messurier: *Keeper of the Old Light,* Western Morning News, 21.09.1964

The Lighthouse was built in 1819, designed by Daniel Alexander, and built by Joseph Nelson. It is of considerable architectural interest, with a tower of cavity construction having double granite walls. The lantern was protected by curtains, and there was a chimney to release the fumes from the oil lamps. Workmen were sent every four years to repaint the lighhouse throughout, and the outhouses and boundary walls were all whitewashed regularly.

The two assistant keepers and their families occupied the main building; the principal keeper's house on the right was dismantled sometime after the new lighthouses were completed in 1897. The families cultivated the gardens in the adjoining paddock and grew their own vegetables.

After 1897 the Lighthouse was leased to a Mr Napier Miles, who used it as a residence for holidays until 1907. He employed a Mr and Mrs Williams as caretakers, who lived in Stoneycroft.

The Lighthouse between 1893–1897.

Trinity House men and their wives at the Fog Signal Station (Battery)

The most likely date for this photograph is 1897, in which case it shows Mr and Mrs Banner, and Mr and Mrs Paul and baby (Margaret).

The Trinity House families were included in the occasional picnics and tea parties given for the Heaven family employees or their children, and they looked to the family for medical help when it was needed. The family paid regular calls at the Lighthouse and Battery, and it is recorded that the ladies rode down the steep path to the Battery and that the horses jumped the last few steps to the houses.

There were thirteen people living in the two cottages at one time and on one occasion when the Elder Brethren came on an inspection, some of the children were sent away to hide until the gentlemen had gone.

In the very severe winter of 1891 there was a heavy fall of snow, and the inhabitants of the Battery were unable to dig out the path, but had to scramble their way up the sideland. The cottages and the guiding wall down to them were whitewashed.

Firing a rocket at the Fog Signal Station, about 1890

The Fog Signal Station was built in 1863 to supplement the Lighthouse, which was frequently obscured by mist. Both continued in use until the new North and South Lighthouses were completed in 1897.

Originally the two guns were used to fire a round of blank shots every ten minutes during fog, but after 1879 guncotton rockets were used instead, as complaints were made that the gunshot intervals were too long for effective warning.

The Castle

The Castle was completed in 1244, after the Mariscos had left the island, as a stronghold constructed by order of King Henry III to prevent Lundy's falling into the hands of rebels. The date of the present keep is disputed. It was examined by Mr C. Winmill (of the Society for the Protection of Ancient Buildings) in 1928, and he was of the opinion that it dated from the 13th century, but he could find no worked stone by which to date it with certainty. Others consider that the building dates from the 17th century. In 1660 Thos. Bushell, who had held Lundy for Charles I during the Civil War, claimed that he "built the castle from the ground at his own charge, fit for any noble person to inhabit."*

In 1752 the keep was inhabited by Benson's convicts, and later both Sir Vere Hunt and William Hudson Heaven housed their labourers in cottages built within it. Recently the keep has been restored by the Landmark Trust, and three cottages have been built into the interior.

The little seat on the south side of the building was put there by the Revd. Heaven and George Thomas in 1879.

The Old House, the remains of which can be seen in the foreground, has recently been excavated, and is judged to date from Bushell's occupation (between 1643 and 1648).†

* *Petitionary Remonstrance*, T. Bushell: 1663
† *National Trust Archaeological Survey*, 1989

The cottages inside the Castle, 1896

The first is taken from the entrance steps looking east, the second looking towards the entrance, and they show the accuracy of the recent restoration by the Landmark Trust.

The baby is Miss Eileen Heaven.

There were three cottages, which housed employees of Mr Heaven. After the Quarry Company had left the island other dwelling houses were available, and the Castle cottages were not fully occupied. They were used for many years by the fishermen and their families who came for the season from Sennen, and were also used from time to time to house shipwrecked sailors or stranded visitors.

The North face of the Castle, 1894

This photograph was taken before the Telegraph Cable Hut was built. The blocked in old doorway can be seen behind the workmen who are sitting down. The man standing on the right was Lloyd's employee on the island, Mr Woods.

The Castle, Cable Hut and Signal Hut, 1906

The Cable Hut

The Cable Hut was built for the G.P.O. in 1894 when the new cable had been provided. Telephone connections were made at this time to the Store, the Villa, the Bungalow, and the Lighthouse, and in 1898 to the post office in Signal Cottages.

Mr Gade says* that the hut had "provision for four men to sleep in bunks, and also a small cooking stove, a wash-basin, a table, chairs, a bench, and some pigeon holes for the sorting of mails." The point of entry of the cable can still be seen. In 1959 the building was extended and converted into a letting cottage for holiday visitors, and re-named "Castle Cottage".

* *My Life on Lundy*, F.W. Gade, 1978

Lloyd's Signal Hut was erected in 1884. About 1959 it was repaired with a flat roof, and housed two bunks which were available for renting in conjunction with any of the holiday cottages. During the winter of 1977–78 the hut was so badly damaged by gales that it had to be demolished.

The flagstaff belonging to the Signal Station is seen on the right of the photograph; the flagstaff on the left, with a weathervane, carried Lloyd's flag. The centre staff was for the semaphore (1893).

Signal Cottages, 1906

Signal cottages were built in 1885 to house Lloyd's employees, and when this photograph was taken they were both occupied by Mr and Mrs Allday, who are seen with their daughter, Mildred. The post office was moved here from the store when Mr Allday was appointed postmaster in 1898. The window of the post and telegraph office is seen bottom left.

This was built by the Admiralty in 1909 as a lookout-station and the telephone was connected. The enclosing fence, the semaphore, kitchen extension and the roof-top observation room have all been removed, and the house now serves as a letting cottage.

The origin of the name "Tibbetts" is not known, but Tibbet's Hill is marked on the Trinity House map of 1820.

Tibbetts from the south-east, 1920

Photo H.W. Jukes

Practice with the Rocket Life-Saving Apparatus about 1900

There are references in the Heaven diaries to Mr Williams coming to Lundy to carry out inspection and rocket practice in 1871, but in September of that year the apparatus was removed as there were not sufficient men on the island for crew after the Granite Company had left. The R.S.L.A. apparatus was installed and the Rocket House built in 1894, after which regular practices were held, supervised by the Commander of Coastguard at Ilfracombe.

The life-saving teams are distinguished by their belts and armbands. The lower picture shows the method of transporting survivors ashore on the rope carried by the rocket to the distressed ship.

The Reredos

The reredos was the work of Harry Hems of Exeter, and shows The Passover, The Last Supper, and The Scapegoat in the Wilderness. Many of the fittings and furnishings were gifts from members of the Heaven family and their friends.

The name of St Helena was probably chosen to maintain continuity while distinguishing this church from the iron church of St Helen. The burial ground and church site were given to the Ecclesiastical Commissioners with land for an adjoining parsonage, but there were no funds available and the house was never built.

The Church soon after completion

The church of St Helena was completed in 1897 and it represented the achievement of the Revd. Hudson Heaven's life-long ambition to see a consecrated building on Lundy. The church can accommodate 165 people. In 1865 the population had been about 240; when the church was completed there were still over sixty inhabitants, who were not infrequently joined by the crews of ships anchoring in the Bay.

The roof was covered with stone tiles which were encrusted with beautiful small fossilised seashells; many of these are now embedded in the path below the bay window in the new tavern.

Lundy had been regarded as extra-parochial, and the patronage assumed by the owner. The Revd. Hudson Heaven became Curate in 1864, and had the courtesy title of Vicar from 1886. He retired in 1911 and was followed by the Revd. William Swatridge as Curate from 1913–16. When the Revd. Heaven died he bequeathed the right of appointment to the Bishops of Exeter. When Lundy has been without a priest, lay readers have conducted services, and among these were William Hudson Heaven and Walter C.H. Heaven.

Sylvia, Leonard and Eileen Heaven at the entrance to Benson's Cave with nursemaid, 1896.

The entrance has since been reduced in height by the accumulation of deposits on the ground.

The structure above the cave was erected to provide a pulley system whereby materials could be transported to and from Lametor during the construction of the South Light.

Entrance to Benson's Cave

The Punchbowl, 1889

It is shown here in its original position, and unbroken. In September 1892 it is recorded that the Punchbowl had been tipped over "by unknown hands" and broken into three pieces. Obviously it was too heavy to have been dislodged by accident. The suspects in cases of depredation, poaching and egg-stealing were usually the crews of tugs or steamers, but there was difficulty in establishing guilt and finding the culprits.

The Punchbowl was repaired, but by 1948 it had been moved and broken again and was repaired by islanders and members of the Lundy Field Society. Absolutely nothing is known of the origin and purpose of this stone; it has been suggested that it may have been connected with corn grinding. It is perhaps worth mentioning that at the head of Punchbowl Valley, on the north side, there is a rough circle of widely-spaced boulders, and traces of walls.

Herding cattle in the Shippons, 1909

Lundy before 1925 was described as "more or less just a farm". Milk was so plentiful that considerable quantities of butter were exported.

Mr George Taylor
Western Mail, c. 1906

Mr Taylor leased the island (except for the Heaven reserve) for £300 p.a. He lived at Abbotsham and came across once a month by the *Devonia* or his own yacht. It was said that he "missed no opportunity of turning a penny" – he increased the number of pleasure steamers and was the first to charge landing fees. He advertised lunch for 2s. and a boarding house with 17 bedrooms. In the Heaven diaries he is referred to as 'Imperator Rex Gubernator' – emperor, king, governor – and it was considered that the island itself was neglected.

In 1909 his successor, Mr Saunt, tried to work up 'The Manor Farm Hotel' and employed as manager a Mr St Claire, who published a guide book and postcards of Lundy. St Claire was bankrupt in 1910, and was found to have retreated to the island under an assumed name to avoid pressure from his creditors.

Mr F. W. Allday and his donkey

The postmaster's duty was to collect and deliver the postbag on the beach.
Mr Wright was responsible for contracting the G.P.O. to serve Lundy. The service started on 4 March 1887, the post office was in the Store, was open from 9–10 a.m. and 5–6 p.m., and postal orders were sold. The sub-postmaster was Mr Wright, who would have deputed the duties to his storekeeper. The enterprise was beset with problems: firstly, the mails were sent weekly by ship from Cardiff, which made for confusion with items sent to the usual address at Instow, especially as Capt. Dark still carried the Heaven letter box. On 16 March the *Queen of the Bay* brought back to the island the mailbag which had been sent off 10 days before, and another time arrived with an incoming bag that had been one week aboard. Another problem was the arrival of the boats in the early hours of the morning with hootings to get attention. Lastly, it was not popular in that the mailbag exchange was such that no time was allowed to send replies by return. From 4 May 1888 Capt. Dark took over the G.P.O. mail contract from Instow.

M. Langham: 'Lundy Post During the Ownership of the Heaven Family',
The Puffin Journal No 26 1983.

The date of origin of the limekiln is not known; the first reference to it in the diaries is in 1871, when the lime was "being done". Mrs M.C. Heaven wrote that as children she and her brother used to cook limpets on the hot stones at the top of the Limekiln.

The lime was imported and burnt in the kiln for use as fertiliser; lime was also used in mortar. The 1906 sale brochure states that the limekiln was capable of turning out about 20 bushels in 24 hours, and that the tenant had joint right of use with the owner.

The limekiln was situated immediately to the south of the cave on the Quay, and it was destroyed in a landslip in 1954.

Photo A.F. Langham, 1951

The Limekiln on the Quay

The Stone

This stone used to be on the Quay, next to the Limekiln, and was lost in the landslip of 1954.

It is not known when, or by whom, it was put there. It read: THIS ISLAND IS ENTIRELY PRIVATE PROPERTY THERE ARE NO PUBLIC ROADS FOOTPATHS OR RIGHTS OF WAY WHATEVER HEREON.

Photo: A.F. Langham, 1953

H.M.S. Montagu

The battleship was wrecked on 30 May 1906, during thick fog, and subsequently the commanding officer and navigating officer were court-martialled and severely reprimanded.

The salvage contractors had workmen living on Lundy, and the suspension bridge seen in the second picture was constructed to provide the men with access to the wreck.

There was a lively trade in steamer trips to view the wreck: the Red Funnel boats (which usually sailed on Tuesdays) made a trip every day, sometimes twice a day, and the *Brighton* also took trippers across. The passengers were not usually landed on the island, but it was possible for islanders and visitors to be conveyed to and from the island in the steamers by arrangement. The island was "swarming with photographers" immediately after the event.

At that time the island was up for sale by auction and a catalogue was prepared. The Revd. Mr Batson offered £30,000, which was accepted, but the sale was not completed, possibly because it was found that possession of the wrecked ship was not included. Other offers were received, but the island was not sold. It is described as "Unique in its rights, privileges and immunities" and "Since there is no question as to the quality of the granite and the supply is practically unlimited, there seems little doubt that an immense fortune awaits anyone with the means to deal with the matter properly."

Dismantling the Montagu

Ladder at Montagu Steps, 1920

About this time landslides made the West Side landing at Pilot's Quay too dangerous to use. Mr Christie therefore had these steps fixed near the place north of Shutter rock where H.M.S. *Montagu* struck, when the weather made a landing on the beach impossible. The photograph was taken at low water by H.W. Jukes.

Lundy Island Post Office, 1925 (The Cable Hut)
Photo: Peter Thomas

This shows Mr Allday, postmaster, outside the post office with the mailbag (which in those days was not secured by a lock). The post office was moved from Signal Cottages to this building in 1909.

Mr Allday joined the Royal Navy when he was 15 years of age, and served in sailing ships. He went to Lundy as Lloyd's signalman in 1896 and did not leave until he went to Ilfracombe to consult a doctor in 1920. He was in charge of the Signal Station until the Admiralty coastguards took over in 1909, Church custodian from 1911, Lloyd's sub-agent from 1918, and postmaster until 1926, when he left the island. Mr Allday told Mr A.E. Blackwell that he had had a donkey to carry the mailbag up from the beach, but that this animal used to make off as soon as the mail boat came into sight and would not return until Mr Allday arrived, perspiring, at the post office.

In 1918, after the Heaven family had sold the island, Mr Allday was admitted as lay reader to the Church of St. Helena, and he regularly conducted services on the island. His daughter, Mildred, married William Thomas on Lundy, which was the first wedding to take place on the island. Their sons lent this photograph.

Landing agricultural machinery, c. 1919

Standing on the ladder is Miss Grace Balley, of Ilfracombe. Across the background is the cable for the South Light hoist.

Drawing by John Dyke
*By permission of Brian Le Messurier** *

This model of the Old Light was presented to Mr McCarthy after he left Lundy in 1893.

The outhouses were built for storerooms, wash-houses and latrines. The water supply was taken from the well, which is still in place.

* B. Le Messurier: *Life on Lundy 100 Years Ago*
North Devon Heritage No 4, 1992

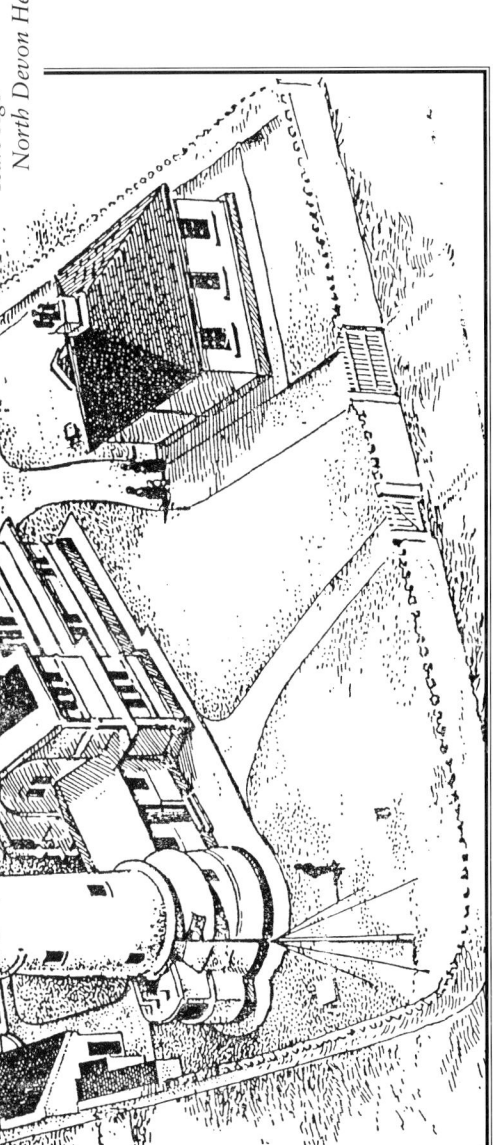

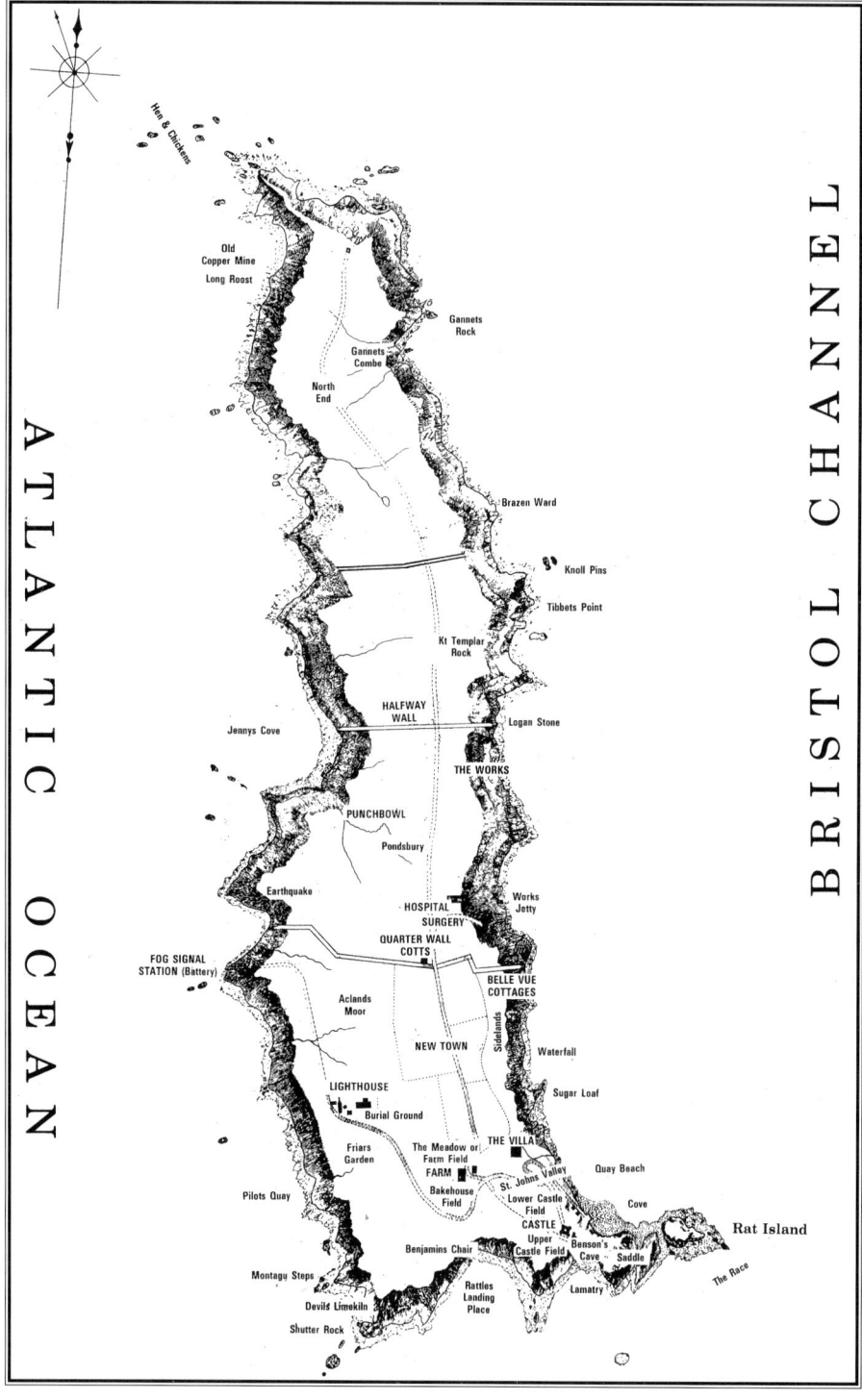

ATLANTIC OCEAN

BRISTOL CHANNEL

Hen & Chickens

Old
Copper Mine

Long Roost

Gannets
Rock

Gannets
Combe

North
End

Brazen Ward

Knoll Pins

Tibbets Point

Kt Templar
Rock

HALFWAY
WALL

Jennys Cove

Logan Stone

THE WORKS

PUNCHBOWL

Pondsbury

Earthquake

Works
Jetty

HOSPITAL
SURGERY

QUARTER WALL
COTTS

FOG SIGNAL
STATION (Battery)

BELLE VUE
COTTAGES

Aclands
Moor

Sidelands

NEW TOWN

Waterfall

LIGHTHOUSE

Sugar Loaf

Burial Ground

THE VILLA

Friars
Garden

The Meadow or
Farm Field

FARM

Quay Beach

Pilots Quay

Bakehouse
Field

St Johns Valley

Lower Castle
Field

Cove

CASTLE

Rat Island

Upper
Castle Field

Benson's
Cave

Benjamins Chair

Saddle

The Race

Montagu Steps

Rattles
Landing
Place

Lamatry

Devils Limekiln

Shutter Rock